ETERNAL SONG

by

Albert C. Clerc

The Ascension at Bethany (Luke 24:50—51)

Counterpoint Publishing Company
Spring, Texas

ETERNAL SONG

First Edition

Library of Congress Catalog Card Number 90-085485

ISBN 1-878149-02-4

Printed in the United States of America

by

COUNTERPOINT PUBLISHING COMPANY
6318 Craigway Road
Spring, Texas 77389
(713) 376-7613

Dedication

To the Divine Poet
whose word has spoken us into existence and who gave me the heart and talent for writing.

To my father, Milton C. Clerc,
who gave me a love for poetry.

To my mother, Flo Nell Jones Clerc,
who gave me the sensitivity and assurance of her love.

To my daughter, Ana Kristin Clerc,
also a budding poet.

To my son, Nicholas Clerc,
who through these words may come to know me as I really am.

And to all the friends
who have given me their support and encouragement.

Contents

Contents

The Annunciation to Mary by the Angel Gabriel (Luke 1:26—38)

I PRAY NOT FOR WEALTH

I pray not for wealth, I pray not for honours, I pray not for pleasures, or even the joys of poetry. I only pray that during all my life I may have love: that I may have pure love to love thee.

Chaitanya, an Indian Mystic

VERMILLION

What wonder in the darkening sky,
What light in shadows shine!
What flowers bloom in shimmering sight,
To battle gloom of gathering night,
What shades like reddened wine!

Now stillness gathers in the sky
And darkness all surrounds.
The moon arises in the east,
To foil the fearful midnight beast,
And softened light abounds.

Two souls reflected in the glass,
Absorbed in fond embrace.
As each to each in silence speaks,
Touching like petals the other's cheeks,
Communing face to face.

TRANSCENDENCE

Transcendence

Presence

Immanent

Intimate

I am one

With you

With Jesu

We are one

A trinity of persons

United in our pain

Our love

Our death

Our resurrection

WHISPERS

Faint wisps of smoke,
Fainter still the fading light,
Faintest whispers of the night.

GIGUE

O dance the dance of life,
The dance that sings within your sinews,
Resonates within the chambers of your heart,
The dance that makes the body sing.

O sing the song of life,
Welling up within your eyes,
Electric bodies singing rhapsodies,
Moving in harmonic communion.

O sing the song and dance the dance,
The God of song and dance
Sings each of us as song
And calls us to the dance of life.

TRUST IN GOD'S PROVIDENCE

My Lord God,
I have no idea where I am going.
I do not see the road ahead of me.
I cannot know for certain where it will end.
Nor do I really know myself,
And the fact that I think that I am following
 your will does not mean that I am
 actually doing so.
But I believe that the desire to please you
 does in fact please you.
And I hope I have that desire
 in all that I am doing.

I hope that I will never do anything apart
 from that desire.
And I know that if I do this,
You will lead me by the right road though I
 may know nothing about it.
Therefore will I trust you always though I
 may seem lost and in the shadow
 of death.
I will not fear, for you are ever with me,
And you will never leave me to face my
 perils alone.

Thomas Merton

SHADOW MAN

In deepening shadows,
I see you there so ill-defined,
Engulfed in pine scent
Like an icon in a niche of smoky night
Frozen by your fear of life.

I call you not with commanding voice,
But softly slowly calling,
Sending my heart into your darkness.
There its heart-glow softly illumines,
Pulsing there within your hand,
Thawing the ice within your being,
Lighting up your shadowed eyes.

LORD, WHERE SHALL I FIND YOU?

Lord, where shall I find you?
High and hidden is your place.
And where shall I not find you?
The world is full of your glory.

I have sought your nearness,
With all my heart I called you
And in going out to meet you
I found you coming in to meet me.

Judah Halebi

THEOTOKOS

You asked me if I think it vain,
Profane to think that you could be
The mother of the chosen one
And I reply that you must be,
For so you're called
To bear anew
The chosen child
Enflesh him in a crying world,
Indeed a dying world.

SECOND INNOCENCE

The wonder of it all,
That I, near half-a-hundred years,
Am still a babe
Within the deep recesses of my mind.
Yet still I wince and cry—
I laugh with child-like joy,
And once again I am a boy.
The wonder of life's stage,
That at my age
I'm all that I have ever been
And all that I will ever be.

There's not just one of me to love
And be loved
By Him who loves me
As I am and was and will be.

A TIME FOR JOY

There is no time that is not meant for joy.
The heart at heaven leaps to break the strain
Of mortal bonds that would the soul employ
In mundane toil to call it down again.

The earth in all its beauty sings a song
That resonates upon the list'ning ear—
The melody of life that flows along
Announcing heaven's joy for all to hear.

And yet preoccupied with things of earth,
Our eyes transfixed by transitory gold,
We starve our souls of things of greater worth . . .
The joys that elevate the attentive soul.

KNOWING AND LOVING GOD

My God, I love thee, not because
I hope for heaven thereby,
Nor yet because who love thee not
Are lost eternally.

Thou, O my Jesus, thou didst me
Upon the cross embrace;
For me didst bear the nails and spear
And manifold disgrace.

And griefs and torments numberless
And sweat and agony;
Even death itself—and all for one
Who was thine enemy.

Then why, O blessed Jesus Christ,
Should I not love thee well;
Not for the sake of winning heaven
Or of escaping hell;
Not with the hope of gaining aught,
Nor seeking a reward:
But as thyself has loved me,
O ever-loving Lord!

Even so I love thee, and will love
And in thy praise will sing,
Solely because thou are my God
And my Eternal King.

Saint Francis Xavier

EXTÁSE

O God creating out of love,
Joyfully creating—
So full of love
Creation springs from you
Spontaneously,
Bountiful, lavish,
Unable to be contained,
As water gushing from a fountain
As flowers budding from the earth.
In wild abandon, you create.
You speak a word of love,
Not quietly,
But passionately,
Exuberantly,
Rapturous,
Ecstatic
Utterance,
Shouting joyfully.

Like a young man
Drunk with love,
Unable to contain his joy,
I speak of you!
My word becomes a song!
It sings in me,
Until I am intoxicated!
It sings in rapturous delight!
It makes my heart
Dance in me.
It overflows like fountains!

I sing of you,
Of my beloved,
And I am drunk
With love!
Like David dancing before the ark.

PILGRIMAGE

I walk and walk,
Until I walk enough—
A pilgrimage to find myself.
I walk three miles a day
And I become the path,
Now in communion with the sky,
The stars and all around,
A peace, intense and yet so light,
Sublime,

My body, my humanity,
The cross I take up daily
Sweet communion with my Christ
My body, God incarnate,
Not deifying me but him,
Who is my flesh, my bone,
My life's blood.

A PRAYER OF AN INDIAN CHRISTIAN

O Tree of Calvary,
Send your roots deep down
Into my heart.
Gather together the soil of my heart,
And sands of my fickleness,
The mud of my desires.
Bind them all together,
O Tree of Calvary,
Interlace them with thy strong roots,
Entwine them with the network
of thy love.

EASTER MORNING

O brilliant day
On which the world was born—
Day on which the Lord has come!

You sing like shimmering brass,
And all creation joins in chorus,
Singing praise,
Singing joyfully to the Lord who made us.

Your song resonates,
Echoing in my soul,
And I become the song.

My spirit sings within me,
Beholding the Lord
In robes of shining white
In glory in the sky.

PIED BEAUTY

Glory be to God for dappled things—
For skies of couple-colour as a brinded cow;
For rose-moles all in stipple upon trout that swim;

Fresh-firecoal chestnut-fall; finches' wings;
Landscapes plotted and pieced-fold, fallow, and plow;
And all trades, their gear and tackle and trim.

All things counter, original, spare, strange;
Whatever is fickle, freckled (who knows how?)
With swift, slow; sweet, sour; adazzle, dim;
He fathers-forth whose beauty is change:
Praise Him.

Gerard Manley Hopkins

SEA GULLS' WINGS

Earth-bound our spirits soar,
We yearn for sea gulls' wings and more
To rise above the shadowed clouds,
To see the sun above the ocean's roar.

Our urgent flesh demands lust food and drink,
Yet all along we stand on sheol's brink.
Some part of us within cannot be stilled—
Will not be bound, must strain at the link

Of chains that bind us to the earth—
That tell us we're of little worth,
Declare to us our mortal fate,
Deny to us the truth of spirit birth.

And yet in exile from our own we know
Reality surpassing earthly show.
Our destiny to die and live no more
But into life's unending tide we flow.

REJOICE

Rejoice in the moment,
The very moment
When you discovered, uncovered,
Like a precious gem,
A "pearl of great price,"
That precious moment,
Radiant, warm,
When it became known to you,
That you were used,
An instrument,
A loving vessel,
A sacrament
To another,
A human being.
A soul used by God,
Not like an inanimate tool
Nor a dumb animal,
But used as a willing,
Giving,
Loving
Instrument of God.

CHRIST HAS NO BODY NOW BUT YOURS

Christ has no body now but yours,
No hands but yours,
No feet but yours.
Yours are the eyes with which he blesses all the world,
Yours are the feet with which he walks about to do good.

St. Teresa of Avila

TERESA'S SONG

O God, incarnate in my flesh,
In the morning of my days,
You wooed me and you won me,
And I have given you my yes,
Not knowing how you gave it power,
Not knowing how you would conjure
To steal that yes and use it.
Still in the silence of my mind,
You stole that yes away and blessed it,
Blessing those who gave their yes,
Saying yes in their unknowing.

You took this yes when even I
was saying yes to tentative urgings of my flesh.
You took this yes and made it shine in me.
I stand in awe that you could take this yes,
This weakly silent yes.
You took this yes and made of it a blessing,
Blessing those with eyes to see,
Blessing those with eager ears to hear,
Blessing those with mouths who said their yes.

I say with joy,
to you my lover, God,
Transcendent,
Immanent,
Intimate God,
I say to you again my yes,
Yes with my mouth, my heart, my eyes,
Yes with my secret body.
I say to you my yes!
O yes!
O yes!

GRAIL PRAYER

Lord Jesus,
I give you my hands to do your work.
I give you my feet to go your way.
I give you my eyes to see as you do.
I give you my tongue to speak your words.
I give you my mind that you may think in me.
I give you my spirit that you may pray in me.

Above all,
I give you my heart that you may love in me,
Your Father, and all mankind.
I give you my whole self that you may grow in me,
So that it is you, Lord Jesus,
Who live and work and pray in me.

PRODIGAL

I run to you and slowly creep away
Until, alone in the desert of my will
I thirst and hunger for your love—
Loving not myself,
Seeing nothing loveable,
My dryness in despair.

How hard it is to turn—
To turn and rise again,
To turn and face you,
To turn and see your love for me,
To see myself reflected in your eyes.

Untarnished,
Unstained,
No longer outcast
But forgiven—
To see me in your eyes,
Loveable
And
Loved.

ETERNAL SONG

O bountiful God,
Lavish as with the waters of the earth
Teeming with life,
Abundant, overflowing!
You sing and life becomes!
Life is in your song,
Life is your song,
Generous, enthusiastic God
Like sparkling springs, you bubble.

O joyous song of God!
Inseminating, impregnating
All creation with your life.

O song of life,
O intimate song,
Permeating,
Quickening the flesh you have created.

How can we contain such joy, such life
Except if we become as God,
Become as you,
To contain all that you are,
To hold all that we might become.

Endless song,
Singing in my being,
Singing me into eternity.

Eternal song of life,
O pregnant song,
Let me be your song,
O intimate loving God.

Withhold for a moment your song,
That I may bear it.

Then resume again—
Let your song ravish me,
Enfold me,
Mold me, weave me, woo me.

Enraptured, I become your song,
O song of songs,
Very song of my being.

I am content, yet discontent.
I am your song without end.
Yet I am the song,
Almost unable to bear it.
Until it ends.

Bear me away O Lover-God!
Make me one with you,
Let no part of me remain
Secret from you.
Invade and conquer all of me.
I surrender and surrender
Saying yes with recklessness.

AFTER THE EVENING RAIN

Through open doors,
I see the shadowed skies,
A timeless scene,
Recalled through wistful eyes.

Somehow the friend I knew
Is now no longer there,
And yet a presence felt
In warm and pensive air.

A closeness I recall,
I could not know,
Would fix this time in me
And never let it go.

On cedar shakes the rain,
Like tears new-wept
Evokes a memory
Which my soul kept.

OASIS

Like an oasis,
A respite from the summers heat,
The morning came,
Fresh and new,
A breeze like spring water
Cool and quenching
Gave a new breath of life.

We are like flowers,
Wilted by the heat of life,
Refreshed by the spring of God's love.

SEASCAPE

The vastness of the summer sky
The vastness of the sea
Is sometimes in a mystic way
Comforting to me.

Its vastness makes my worries small
It gives me clarity.
To see how transient is the day
How lost in its immensity.

Somehow a calm befalls my life
When I am at the sea
And when I gaze at summer skies
Somehow it sets me free.

STILL POINT

Death,
Like a petal falling,
Softly,
Imperceptibly,
Lights upon the snow.
In candlelight
I reach for a still point
Becoming who I am.

PRAYER FROM KENYA

From the cowardice that dares not face new truth,
From the laziness that is contented with half-truth,
From the arrogance that thinks it knows all truth,
Good Lord, deliver me.

AUTUMN TIDE

There is somehow a turning point,
imperceptible,
Some change of the tide of day
When, without significant variation,
A consciousness rises
That autumn is near.

It is as subtle as a whispered sigh,
That to the inattentive ear
Remains unnoticed.

Yet to my soul
That sends out sentinels
Spying for its initial signs,
It is a distant trumpet
Heralding golden moments
And days of soft reflection.

l(a
le
af
fa
ll
s)
one
l
iness.

e. e. Cummings

PSALM-DE PROFUNDIS

Like wind bereft of warmth,
My soul, my heart, my being,
Bereft of love,
Of the touch of another being,
Lies desolate like a fallen leaf,
Decayed and brown and dead.

Even the sunshine's warmth
Does not revive my spirit.
How can I rise above
This gray and dreary landscape?
How can I hope for love—
I who have shuttered my soul?

A quiet spring must bubble
Deep in despair's dark depths.
There, I must slake this longing
That empties my soul of spirit.

Outward I must move—
Not sleep nor crouch in darkness.
In stone I must carve this mandate,
"Seek the warmth of love within.
If not found then seek its shadow—
Seek its ever faintest traces."

CORNUCOPIA

Sometimes a clarity of mind
Comes like a northern wind,
Shines like the sun on a winter's day,
Brightens the heart with hope.
And with that hope,
I am one with sun,
I become the wind,
All things are possible.

My heart
Like a horn of plenty,
Overflows with abundant fruit.
I am fertile with joy.

Ideas within my mind,
Joy within my soul,
Are like sweet fruit,
Cool and refreshing
To the taste.
You Lord are the joy of my heart.
You are the brightness within my soul.
You make all things possible.

THERE IS A LONGING IN THE HEART

There is a longing in the heart,
A void that grows in autumn
Like a ripening pumpkin,
Growing golden on the vine,
Calling us home
To the harvesting of our joys—
Home to the nest where we belong.

Our hearts fly ahead of us,
Reaching out
Like migratory birds—
Longing for that home
From all the trials of life.

Deep inside something in us sings
A longing song,
Echoing Augustine, who said,
"O God our hearts are made for thee
And they shall not rest
Until they rest in thee."

TRYST

I feared His "yes"—
I feared as well His "no."
I feared to stay
But feared far more to go.
To see Him there
Now hanging on the tree,
Made my heart freeze
And jelled the fear in me.
He seemed to ask
If I would follow Him.
To me the task
Seemed difficult and grim.
And I was made
Of weaker stuff than this—
He softly cried
Then sealed me with a kiss.
Then weak of knee—
No will of mine but His,
I climbed the tree
To find no earthly bliss,
But only Love
Found nailed onto a tree—
The stuff I lacked
To seal my Love with me.

NATIVITY

This gift of days,
Of childhood days,
A waiting in the heart,
Anticipation of a time,
Opening like a flower,
Joy in the hope of blooming,
Renewal and rebirth of hope.

In the deep stillness of the night,
The candlelight of stars
Whispers a pregnant stillness,
Waiting to be born in us,
Hope anew with brightly opening eyes.

TEENAGERS' PRAYER FROM HARARE, ZIMBABWE

God, help me to be human. Help me to be able to appreciate and bring out the best in everyone around me. You have created man, so that he is capable to appreciate consciously all the gifts that you have given him. Lord, help me to appreciate all you have given me. Help me to be truly human.

GIFT

You have given me myself—
And for that gift,
That precious gift of self
O Lord,
I am truly thankful.
Your song sings in me
And I am lyrical,
Singing to myself,
To you
To whom I belong,
To whom I give myself
In sweet abandon.

You have given me myself—
I give myself to you again.

APERITIF

What mind
That sips the draught of death,
Cold and bittersweet,
Inviting to the taste,
Or chill and terrible,
Distills within that final moment,
Insights,
Intense in their reality,
Tasting truth.

Could we but know that truth,
Would we not see with clearer eyes,
And then drink deep
The draught of life.

INNER STRENGTH

Let me not pray to be sheltered from dangers
But to be fearless in facing them.

Let me not be for the stilling of my pain
But for the heart to conquer it.

Let me not crave in anxious fear to be saved
But hope for the patience to win my freedom.

Grant me that I may not be a coward,
Feeling your mercy in my success alone;
But let me find the grasp of your hand in my failure.

Rabindranath Tagore

REFLECTION I

The reality of life,
measured in seconds,
no yesterday or tomorrow.
There is but now in which to live.

REFLECTION II

In the stillness of the evening shadows,
silence swells to a fullness,
Filling the sky with love.

Holy is this moment—
caught between day and night.

My heart is filled with your silence,
your stillness wells up within me.

You, Lord, make me giddy,
intoxicated,
overwhelmed by your love.

How we are entwined O Lord,
how we are intermingled,
your people and I.

FACT OF LIFE

We live illusions, living lies,
Until the ultimate surprise.
The pain cuts deep and then we see
The ultimate reality.

Alone in darkness still we cry,
In rage denying that we die.
We die alone until we see
The ultimate reality.

And dying alone in darkness blind.
Afraid of shadows in our mind.
Alone we cry until we see
The ultimate reality.

Caught up by death's embrace
We see Him face to face.

PRAYER OF ZANDE CHRISTIANS

As tools come to be sharpened by the blacksmith, so may we come, O Lord. As sharpened tools go back with their owner, so may we go back to our everyday life and work, to be used by thee, O Lord.

Acknowledgements

There are many friends who through their support both practical and prayerful have helped me bring this book to fulfillment. To these I wish to express thanks and acknowledgement.

Glenn Currier for his early encouragement of my writing.

Virginia Long and the poets of the Houston Poetry Society.

Ruby Bussey, Ovon Ross and the poets of the San Jacinto Chapter.

Claire Ottenstein, Betty Hurley, Dalphna Barnes and all the poets of Poets Northwest.

To these three groups for so much creative stimulation.

To *Theresa Russo* for being there for me.

To *Marsha Hartl* and *Susan Kohrman* for the mundane chore of typing and re-typing.

To my pastor *Don Neumann* for his encouragement and inspiration.

To *Betty Wall*, my supervisor, for her encouragement and advice on the arrangements of these poems.

To *Jeff* and *Susan Kohrman* for their support when I was in the "valley of the shadow of death."

To any and all of my friends whom I may have forgotten to acknowledge, know that you are acknowledged in my heart and in my prayers.

And to *Edna Steckler* who has through her constant prayers and steadfast discernment encouraged me to finally publish this piece.

The Sower (Matthew 13:3—23)